Copyright

MW01293119

The Key to Making Money On Instagram

How I Make Hundreds Per Post

Dave Wells

Contents

Remember to Checkout my Facebook Page:

Dave Wells

Chapter 1: The Beginning

Making money on Instagram all started for me back when I was still using the app for recreational purposes. At the time, I was following an Instagram page related to super cars that posted photos of Ferraris and corvettes.

One day, I noticed that the page I was following was doing sponsored posts. It was advertising t-shirts, luxury car accessories and even high end wallets. At first I figured that the page was advertising its own products. But as time went on, I realized that the luxury car Instagram page was simply promoting products for companies. Even BMW was using this page to promote its new clothing line.

Out of curiosity I began to do my research, wondering how much these Instagram users were getting paid to post. I contacted several pages, asking if they'd spare me a minute to answer some questions over Skype.

Eventually, I found a guy named Pat, who agreed to Skype me for ten minutes or so. He explained to me that he made $100 every time someone purchased a sponsored post on his page, which at the time had 600k followers.

I then asked him how much time he spent running his Instagram page. The answer? Only 20 minutes each day.

For the time commitment that was a fantastic return! And what was even better was that people with over a million followers, were making $500 plus per post.

After that Skype call, I instantly jumped into the Instagram game, learning everything I possibly could about the platform. It's now my main and greatest source of income, making me over six figures each year.

The best part being that you can run an Instagram page from anywhere. In a coffee shop, in a hotel, and it only takes minutes of your time to post. You don't need to be a master at creating content, or even be an entertaining character. All you need to do is find quality pictures that you can repost.

Chapter 2: The Mindset

Always Expand your Knowledge

To start this book off, I'd like to personally thank you for purchasing my e-book and taking a chance on me to further your knowledge and expand what you know about Instagram. By taking this first step, you have already proven that you are willing to invest in your education. This is a crucial idea that you will have to embrace in order to become successful online. The reason being that the online world of social media is constantly changing. From my experience, the people that make the most money on the Internet, are the ones that are constantly learning and teaching themselves new tricks and techniques to further their business.

So keep that in mind as you begin to make extra income off of social media and the internet. Always set aside a portion of your earnings that you will use to further develop your knowledge and understanding of Internet business and Internet marketing. There's always something new that can be learned, and even the slightest detail can give you the upper edge.

Just to give you an example of this, a friend of mine was making a great deal of money from his Facebook page that he used to target a very specific niche. Using Facebook ads, he quickly grew his business and began making a lot of money selling various health related products to his targeted following. As time went on, the niche that he was targeting started to become more and more saturated, making it harder for him to make a large profit on the products that he was selling. In short, he was forced to shrink his profit margins.

Another friend of mine that I actually met at a conference, was in the same sort of business, using Facebook groups and Facebook ads to sell an arsenal of different products. However, unlike my first friend, he educated himself daily and discovered that there was enormous potential on different platforms besides just Facebook. Using his knowledge, he quickly expanded his business on to Instagram, twitter, Pinterest, and even YouTube.

The two friends both started in relatively the same place. However, one chose to adapt to the changes in the social media realm, making his business triple while the first friends business shrunk.

In the world of online business, it is essential to be constantly expanding, and researching how you can further develop your audience and customers. Now I know this book is about Instagram, but I just want you to keep all of this in mind while you are reading. Instagram is probably the hottest social media platform for making money today, but that doesn't mean that it will always be this way in the future. Furthermore, I predict that Snapchat will in fact dominate in the years to come. With this being said, you should try to use the growth that you will experience on Instagram to build an empire of social media followings, spread across a variety of different networks.

The Instagram Battle

In order to make money on Instagram, you need a large following of people. The more followers that you have, the more money you will make. With that being said, gaining followers on Instagram can be extremely tiresome and gruelling.

Always remember the endgame, and constantly remind yourself why you are doing this in the first place. There will be days during your Instagram journey when you just don't feel like posting, and feel like you are making no progress. This is all part of the process. Gaining a following on Instagram and building up a network of niche related followers is something that requires an insane amount of patience and persistence.

You don't need to necessarily be smart to make money on Instagram, in fact anybody can do it. The skills that you need are only patience and persistence, like I said above. If you have those two qualities, you are more than capable of building accounts that will have over 1 million followers.

The Time Frame

So now that I have explained how difficult this journey is going to be, you are probably wondering how long it is going to take before you start noticing real results on Instagram. Personally, it took me around a year to build a 200,000 follower Instagram page, and 2 1/2 years to build a 1 million follower Instagram page. Once you pass the 1 million follower mark, you will easily be making over $100,000 per year, assuming that a large portion of your followers are engaged.

So if you look at that time frame, you will potentially be making one hundred thousand dollars in a time line of almost 3 years, assuming that you stick with it every single day and never give up. If you think about it, that's not really a long time to go from making zero dollars $100,000. College students have to stay in schools for four years just to get a degree!

Also, once you have a page with 1 million followers, it will be a lot easier for you to grow even more pages and expand on to other social media platforms. I will explain all of this later on in the book, and will teach you how to grow on social media exponentially.

Just keep in mind that the first milestones are always the hardest. The first thousand followers and the first 100,000 followers will always be harder than the next.

Chapter 3: Choosing your Niche

So now that you have a little bit of background information, and a little bit of motivation, let's get right into starting your business on Instagram.

The first step, is to pick your niche. This can be dogs, cats, trucks, travel photos, funny memes, interesting quotes, business quotes etc. just make sure that whatever you choose, you are extremely interested in the subject.

You are going to be working with your niche every single day, so you want to make sure that it's something that you enjoy.

Also, when thinking about your niche it is important to do a little bit of research before jumping right in. You'll want to head over to Instagram and check out how many other pages are in the same niche as you. When looking, you want to make sure that there as at least one other page that has 1 million followers in the same general category. This is because you don't want to pick a niche that people will not be interested in.

An example of a good niche, is trucks, and truck related posts. An example of a bad niche is ice fishing in the Yukon. As much as you may love ice fishing in the Yukon, it's simply not something that the mass public would be interested in. Trucks on the other hand, is a niche that can be expanded upon and broken down into sub niches.

Let's say that for your first Instagram page you decide to create a general trucks fan page. Not a bad idea. From there, once that account starts to grow, you can expand by creating other Instagram pages that focus on Ford trucks, Chevy trucks, and dare I say it

Dodge trucks. The same principle can be applied within an Instagram page about dogs or puppies. Once your main page starts to pick up traction, you can then expand by creating smaller pages focusing on different types of dog breeds such as pugs, German shepherds, or whatever.

The main page, or the general niche page, is what will be bringing in the majority of traffic. The smaller sub niche pages, is what you will use to laser target your followers. Think about how much easier it would be to sell a pug T-shirt to a fan page about pugs rather than a general puppy lovers page.

So just to recap, pick a niche that you love and are interested in, but make sure it's broad enough that you can zoom in on more targeted niches. After you've come up with that niche, write it down on a piece of paper. Now go and do some research. Find out how many other Instagram pages are in the that same niche, and see how many followers they have. The goal is to find a niche with at least one page over 1 million followers, and to find a page that you could outperform with better quality posts.

A lot of the popular Instagram pages these days, are run by people who quite frankly don't care about the quality of their posts. They post blurry pictures and don't even bother to write a caption. Why? Well because they got into the game early. These types of accounts most likely started their fan pages right is Instagram was becoming increasingly popular. I've seen countless pages with millions of followers that post very crappy pictures. Anybody, especially you, can do a better job. So when you find a crappy Instagram page that has over 1 million followers in the niche that you're interested in, you should get very excited.

Keeping the End Game in Mind

When choosing your Instagram niche, it's important to have some sort of end game or end goal in mind. How are you planning to monetize your Instagram page? Are you going to create a web store? Are you going to sell shoutouts? If you're going to sell shoutouts, how many large companies are out there that could potential be interested? Just have some sort of idea.

Most Instagram niches can be monetized in some way shape or form, it's just a matter of discovering what your Instagram followers truly want.

The only niches that are extremely hard to monetize are celebrity fan pages and pages related to specific movies etc. Most of the time, fan pages slowly fade away, and the followers become disinterested with the movie once it has been out for a couple of years. The only Instagram page that I've seen able to monetize in this type of niche was a Harry Potter fan page, and they had a web store selling replica wands for a steep price. Now although this may have been a good idea, you'll want to choose a niche that is long term, something isn't a fad and something that will still be around in ten years.

Chapter 4: Choosing Your Username

Once you've done your research and have a niche in mind, (something you're interested in), it's time to choose a username. Usernames need to be simple, memorable, and straight to the point. The better your username, the more of an advantage you will have on Instagram. Here's some basic guidelines:

Do not use numbers in your username.

Using numbers in your username will only confuse people and will hurt your ranking on Instagram's search. If you start a page called "puppyphotos31" that posts puppy memes, what's to stop someone else from making a page called: "puppyphotos32." It will simply leave everyone very confused. The only exception is if the numbers are directly related to your niche, such as "420humor."

Use your niche's keyword first.

Trucksdaily will always be a more effective username than dailytruckposts. When looking for a username, you want to make sure that your main keyword is first, as that is what people will be searching for.

Underscores are ok if you are separating words.

I actually own an Instagram page with an underscore that gained followers extremely quickly. At first I was skeptical about using an underscore, but it actually proved to be more effective because I could isolate my keyword. Something like trucks_daily is a really good username. Another tip is to try to only use two words when using underscores.
Truck_postsdaily isn't a username that you would want.

Don't make your username too long.

This one isn't a huge deal but if you can, try to pick a username that is short and to the point.

There's no need to stress out about finding the perfect username. You can always change it later on down the road by simply going into your account settings. Also, if you're getting stuck trying to find an available username, try looking at the account names of some of the larger accounts in different niches. This will help you generate some ideas for your specific niche. Here's some examples to get you started:

trucks_daily

truck_domination

trucklover

foodporn

fitness_mentor

yogapostsdaily

cooking_clips

You get the idea. Just try and make sure that the word people will be searching for, is first.

Chapter 5: Setup

After you've secured a username that you feel is worthy of your niche, it's time to begin setting up your page to look as professional as possible. Take your time when choosing a profile picture, a description, and the title of your Instagram page.

It's a good idea to have a custom designed profile picture to match the name of your Instagram page. If you are familiar with Photoshop, you can do this quite easily using their tools. If you don't have Photoshop, you can use pixlr, which is a free and more basic version of Photoshop.

Lastly, if you have no Photoshop skills whatsoever, you can head on over to fiverr.com and pay somebody five bucks to design a custom logo and profile picture for your new Instagram page. If you have a really long username, it might be a good idea not to include your username in the profile photo. Look around at what your competitors are doing, take note of what profile pictures they are using and ask yourself how you can do it better. You want a profile picture that will entice people to click on your Instagram page, something bold that stands out.

If you are starting a truck page, you'll probably want to have the most bad ass truck picture you can find as your profile picture.

When writing the title of your Instagram page, it's important to include your keyword as the first word, just like your username. So if you are running a funny meme's page, the title of the page should be something like: "Humor Daily."

Finally, in the description of your Instagram page, you'll want to write something short and simple about what your Instagram page is all about. Another good idea for your description, is to add some sort of contact information, such as an email address or a kik username. By adding your contact information, you are leaving yourself open to network with other Instagram accounts.

It is also a good idea to get a hashtag started for your Instagram account. You can do this by writing in the description a little snippet that looks something like this:

"Tag #truckpostsdaily to be featured on our page!"

This lets new followers know that if they post a picture of their truck, and use that hashtag, they can be featured and promoted on your page. By doing this, you will increase exposure to your Instagram page, and will also find free content that you can use to post on your Instagram page.

Before getting followers...

Before you go out and hunt for followers, it's important to add some content to your

Instagram page, so that your page doesn't look plain or abandoned. I'd recommend posting at least 10 photos on your page, before you go out and start following people. You'll want these 10 photos to be really unique and eye-catching, so take your time when looking. A great place to look for photos to post on Instagram, is Pinterest and Tumblr. Post something popular that a lot of people already like and have responded to on these other social media websites.

Think of some clever Captions to use with these first photos, and make sure that you use your hashtag with each post. People are not going to want to follow and Instagram page that has no captions, because it looks like you are just a robot automatically throwing pictures out on your Instagram page.

Chapter 6: Gaining

Followers

Finally, after hunting down a username, filling your Instagram page with good quality content and captions, it's time to begin the long process of finding followers.

At first, you will need to reach out to people in some way shape or form. This means following people, liking their photos, commenting on their photos, getting your Instagram page out on different social media, and more! It will be the most time consuming and challenging part of your journey which is why I will make this section of the book the most detailed.

To begin this section, I want to start off by saying that it will be easier to gain followers once you already have a decent following (ten thousand people) which means that for the first bit, you're going to be on the grind to 10k.

The fastest way and cheapest way to gain 10k followers is to start off by following people that you believe will be interested in your page. You can do this all manually, or you can use a bot, that will automatically follow people that are likely to follow your page.

First, I will explain the manual aspect of this process. If you have the time (example sitting bored in class with nothing to do) doing the following process manually will be your fastest option. In fact, if you really wanted to, you could probably gain 10k followers in a week just by manually following people.

So who do you follow?

From my experience, if you are doing everything manually, the best people to follow

are the ones who have recently liked a photo.
I'll give you an example.

Let's say you're starting a page regarding
sports cars. So, in order to gain your first
followers, what you should do is find another
page on Instagram (preferably with over a
million followers) that posts sports car related
posts. The trick is to wait until that page posts
a photo. Within the first hour of the photo
being posted, what you're then going to do is
follow all of the people that have LIKED their
new post. Follow as many of them as you can,
and refresh the image constantly so that you
are following LIVE users that have liked the

sports car related photo within the last couple of seconds.

This is how you INSTANTLY gain followers. Because these people are live, you will be gaining followers extremely quickly.

You can also follow the other Instagram account's followers, however from my experience, following the users that have recently liked one of their photos is the most effective way.

Hashtags

Another great way to gain followers manually is to like photos with a particular hashtag that is directly related to your page. In the case of the car page, you could use a hashtag such as "#sportscar." Go through and like all of the most recently posted photos, as these pictures will have likely been posted within the last couple of minutes, giving you live Instagram users as well.

Gaining Followers Automatically Using a Bot

Ok so what if you don't want to do all this manually? Let's say you're a little more patient, and can tolerate waiting a little longer to get your 10k followers. Well, in that case, I'd highly recommend that you purchase a bot, that can automatically like photos, comment, and follow users. I've used bots to grow all of my Instagram accounts, and have never been banned once from Instagram (fingers crossed.)

If you're going to go the bot route, I must warn you that it is possible for your Instagram account to get banned if you push the limits too much. The key is to keep the bot's settings reasonable, so that you fly under Instagram's radar. I also believe that Instagram isn't looking to ban accounts that are reasonably using bots to gain exposure for their account. In fact, most large pages on Instagram have used a bot at one point or another.

There are many Instagram bots out there, but the only one that I've used is called Followliker. It works flawlessly, has constant updates, and has great customer support. I've never had any trouble with their services, so I'd highly recommend that if you're going to use a bot, to use followliker.

If you want to use a different bot for whatever reason, make sure that the developer has some sort of credibility, otherwise they can simply hack and take your account. I've met and know a lot of large Instagram account users who use followliker, and they've never had a problem with hacks or account stealing. Besides, after you gain around 50k followers or so, there will be no need for you to use follow liker for that certain account, unless you are going to use the bot to automatically post pictures.

Another bonus about followliker is that you can manage multiple Instagram accounts, giving you more diversification when it comes to your niches. I want to point out that you shouldn't run more than FIVE Instagram accounts on followliker at a given time, otherwise you may face a ban from Instagram.

To this day I am running five Instagram accounts with followliker, and have had no issues whatsoever.

In terms of settings with followliker, I keep the activity that the bot does very conservative to avoid raising red flags on Instagram. I also don't use the "follow" and "unfollow" settings at the same time. I wait until the accounts have followed around 1500 people, and then turn off the "follow" setting, and turn on "unfollow." I also don't overdo it with the likes and features of the bot, instead I make all of the settings very realistic.

I could cover all of the settings I use with the program, however there is a fantastic instruction manual/tutorial that comes with the bot when you purchase it. If you're going to invest in one thing for your Instagram journey, I'd recommend investing in followliker. It costs around $70.

Chapter 7: Buying

Instagram Accounts

If you don't want to start an Instagram account from scratch, buying an Instagram account is an option. However, you have to be EXTREMELY careful when it comes to finding an actual and legit Instagram page. I've bought multiple Instagram accounts over the last couple of months, and I've always been extremely diligent when it comes to doing the research.

To start, if you're going to be buying an Instagram account, I'd recommend buying them over a platform that has some sort of safety or insurance behind it, such as Ebay. In fact, all of my Instagram account purchases have been done over Ebay. This is because, Ebay has a buyer protection program, to protect buyers like yourself from scammers and con artists. If you can, try to purchase Instagram accounts from friends or friends of friends. Many of my account purchases were made through someone I know in the Internet marketing realm. The more unknown the person is, the more your money is at risk.

If you're going to buy an account, I'd recommend NOT buying an account with over 50k followers. Accounts that are over 50k followers will be extremely expensive, leaving you at more risk to scammers. Plus, people with large accounts usually know the value of their account, and probably wouldn't be interested in selling in the first place.

Another thing to watch for is fake followers and fake likes. A lot of Ebay Instagram account listings are completely fake accounts, which can leave you bummed and discouraged. These accounts purchase fake followers, likes and comments from websites like fivver.com.

I'd recommend buying an Instagram account in the 10k to 20k follower range. This should cost you anywhere from $50 to $300 depending on how active the users are.

When looking to purchase an Instagram account, there's a number of things that you should check before buying, just to make sure that you aren't buying a fake account. Here's a list:

-*The account should have over 100 posts*

-Check the followers to make sure the majority have profile pictures

-Check the followers and see how many posts they have. Also make sure that they aren't following thousands of people.

-Check for legitimate comments. Some fake accounts have fake likes with no comments.

-Check the selling history of the Ebay seller by clicking on their username. If they have any negative feedback at all, don't do the deal.

Another thing to mention is that you should make the purchase over Ebay. A lot of the time, these eBay listers will try and do the transaction off of eBay, with direct paypal. Do NOT do this, you will lose your buyer protection, which is what the scammers want.

After Purchasing the Account:

As soon as you purchase an Instagram account off of Ebay, you should immediately change the password, email, phone number and perhaps the username if there is numbers in the username.

With every Instagram account I've purchased off of Ebay, I've always remained in the same niche, but changed the username. If the seller doesn't even know your new username, there's no way they could ever regain access to the account.

Chapter 8: Buying

Shoutouts

Purchasing shoutouts is a fantastic way to grow your Instagram account. I recommended not purchasing shoutouts until you have at least 10k followers, since your page will be more attractive once you've gained a following.

To purchase shoutouts, search for Instagram accounts that are in the same niche as yourself, but with more followers. Usually, they'll leave a KIK contact username, or an email address. Simply ask them how much a shoutout is going to cost, and compare the prices with other accounts.

Personally, I've never been scammed when purchasing shoutouts, so don't worry too much about that aspect.

You can find shoutouts for cheap on fiverr.com buysellshoutouts, and even ebay.

What to Post for your Shoutouts

Before purchasing a shoutout, you'll want to test the picture or video on your page first, just to make sure that it's going to be a successful post. What I like to do is take my most commented on photo and use that for my shoutouts that I'm doing with larger accounts.

For your caption, you want it to look as natural and as less spammy as possible. For myself, my most successful captions have been something like:

"Found this hilarious vid on @funnymemes, check them out."

It's simple and informative. If your description

is too long, people might not even bother to

read it. Try to avoid captions like:

FOLLOW @FUNNYMEMES

@FUNNYMEMES

@FUNNYMEMES

@FUNNYMEMES

Honestly, everyone on Instagram does this,

and I can tell you from personal experience, it

doesn't work anymore. People just see that as

spam, and will even be annoyed with your page.

Chapter 9: Growing Your Instagram Empire

Once one of your Instagram pages begins gaining traction, you can use your following to jump start another Instagram page. I'll give you an example.

Let's say you have a puppy page with 100k followers. You've been building this page up for the last 6 months, and have decided that you're ready to start another Instagram page. Try to keep your second Instagram page in the same niche, but make it somewhat different. If you have a puppy page where you post pictures, create a second Instagram account where you post short video clips.

This way, you can give yourself shoutouts. Eventually, once your second Instagram page has been jumpstarted, you won't even need to give it shoutouts anymore, as it will start to grow naturally. I've seen an Instagram page with 500k followers grow a second Instagram page to 200k followers in less than 6 months!

You can literally use this method as a domino effect, and create an absolute empire on Instagram.

Shoutout for Shoutout

A great way to grow your Instagram following is to find accounts that have a similar number of followers as yourself. Message them, email them, and network with them. There are many Internet marketing forums such as blackhatworld where you can find hundreds of Instagram users like yourself.

Building a community and a team of people on Instagram is also a fantastic way to build momentum when growing on Instagram. You'll learn twice as fast, and will make fewer mistakes when it comes to building a large following, and maximizing your profits.

You can find "Instagramers" on Facebook in Facebook groups, forums, youtube, and more. Search around, collect Skype names, and talk Instagram strategy. You'll be surprised how much you'll learn. Set a monthly or weekly skype meeting time, so that you get into the habit of meeting with your team, and growing your team.

From personal experience, I've gained a lot of internet marketing knowledge from simple skype meetings. Business ideas are generated, and everyone in the group benefits immensely. The fastest way to learn, is always by talking to someone directly. Skype enables this.

Chapter 10: Making Money

on Instagram

By now you're probably wondering how all of your hard work is going to pay off. How are you going to monetize your followers and following? Well, there isn't one correct method or way to do this. It really all depends on your niche, your engagement, and what your followers want.

In the next sections of this book, I'll be covering all the ways that I know of to monetize your Instagram account. (You can even use several at the same time!)

This next chapter is going to be absolutely packed full of information. What I'd recommend you do is to read one method a day, and do your own research on each monetization method. Grab a notepad, watch youtube tutorials, read blogs, and research the method until you fully understand it. In order to properly monetize your Instagram page, you're going to need to know all of the options, and pick the best one for your audience.

This book would be extremely long if I went into detail on each method, however I will try to be as concise as possible.

Selling Shoutouts:

This is the most common way to make money on Instagram. The more followers that you have, the more you'll make selling Instagram shoutouts. Personally, I make around $300 a day just selling shoutouts on my different Instagram accounts. And the best part is, I don't need to do much advertising. For the most part, people come to me, asking how much I charge for shoutouts.

I leave my email address and my KIK username in my page's description, and people contact me daily. Because I have many different Instagram accounts, I've created multiple emails for each account, so that I don't get confused. I then set up an auto responder, that will automatically give people my rates, my paypal email, and information. This completely automates the shoutout process. I can literally wake up, check my paypal account, and find people who have paid me to post shoutouts for the day.

When you're just getting started with selling shoutouts, I'd recommend not automating the process at first. Deal with people directly, as you will have a higher conversion rate. The reason why I've made my shoutout process automatic is because I get too many requests anyway, and I don't want to constantly spam my pages with ads and promotions. A good guideline is to only post a maximum of two shoutouts each day, so that you don't anger your followers. The more shoutouts you post, the slower your Instagram account will grow because people tend not to tag their friends on sponsored posts.

If you're just starting out with selling shoutouts, I'd recommend creating a GIG on fiverr.com or creating an eBay listing. This will get people purchasing shoutouts from you even if you only have a small following (10k-50k followers). Once you get an initial base of people buying shoutouts from fiverr, you can make them reoccurring customers off of fiverr through direct messaging and paypal.

Another tip is to make sure you grab each person's email address. Create a mailing list compiled of people that have purchased shoutouts in the past. Each month, offer discounts to everyone on this mailing list, to remind them of your shoutout services. Often times, companies forget about the positive experience that they had with your Instagram account. A friendly email, is a great way to remind them.

Pricing Shoutouts:

How you price your shoutouts and rates generally is based on your niche and the amount of followers you have. Some niches simply have more shoutout demand than others, raising the prices higher. Car and fitness pages for example make much more than a humor page of the same following. This is because it's easier to sell things on car and fitness niches, as the audience is more targeted.

Another tip when selling shoutouts is to include bundle prices. If you normally charge $100 for a 24 hour shoutout, tell your potential buyer that you'll sell them three 24 hour shoutouts for $90 each or five 24 hour shoutouts for $80 each. The more people buy in bulk, the more money you will make in the long run. The reason I'm able to make so much from shoutouts is because I have around 10 companies that buy 5+ bulk shoutouts each month, giving me a solid basis of income.

Reaching Out to Companies

Once you've reached around 200k followers or so, and have a well established Instagram page, it's time to start contacting companies. You'll want to find businesses that are run by their original owner, so that you can contact them directly. Don't try and make deals with massive companies like Walmart or Bestbuy.

You should be looking for small to medium sized companies that are run by one to five people. Online businesses and companies tend to have a higher conversion rate, although local businesses buy shoutouts as well. Try to look for online companies that are selling a specific product that is directly related to your niche. They'll immediately realize the value that your Instagram page can be to their company.

Your goal should be to sell these companies a package of shoutouts (a shoutout each week for a month), for a bulk price. So if you have 250k followers, and sell shoutouts for $100 each, sell the package for $350. Most companies have an advertising budget, and will happily spend $350 each month for some quality advertising.

If you have 10 companies or so buying from you each month, you'll be making $3500 on autopilot. As time goes on, you can raise the prices with these companies, and keep up a good relationship.

When wording your email to these companies, make sure that you include the amount of followers that you have. As soon as the owner sees, "250k niche related followers," they'll instantly become interested. Here's an example of an email:

"Dear (Company Name)

My name is Rick and I'm reaching out on behalf of my Instagram page @puppyphotos. We have 250k followers that all own and love puppies. We think that your product would work really well with our page, and was wondering if you'd be interested in doing some monthly advertising with us. We offer a package deal of 4 featured promotions for $350 a month.

Let me know if you're interested, thanks for your time,

-Rick.

It's important to get the company thinking about monthly rates. If you make it seem like a onetime deal, chances are it will be. You want to get the subscription mentality in the back of their head.

E-Commerce Web Stores:

Web stores definitely have the most potential out of all the money making methods with Instagram. This is because it gives you a chance to build a permanent brand, that could potentially become huge.

Even if Instagram starts to go downhill, with a web store, you will still be making huge profits. I could write an entire book about building a web store and customer base with Instagram, but I'll try to stick to the major points, just to get you started.

For starters, let's talk about what you should sell. The name of the game is to find exclusive products that cater towards your niche and page audience. You need to find something that people can't buy in stores, that they

NEED to buy online. It also helps if it's a viral product. If people are tagging their friends on Instagram when they see a photo of your product, it's a viral product.

Let me give you an example. If you run a puppy/dog page, and you're looking to start a web store, do not sell generic, basic dog collars. Instead, sell custom made GPS tracking dog collars that allow you to track your puppy from your phone. Create a brand and build a website around this specialty product, giving you a monopoly amongst all other competition.

So how do I find these exclusive products?

Checkout alibaba.com. They have pages and pages of incredible products that you've probably never seen before. The best part being that they give you the chance to custom brand the products that they've designed with your logo.

All you need to do is go to the search bar, and look up the keyword of your Instagram page. You'll find hundreds of extremely cool products that have the potential to go viral. From there, email or call the supplier, and ask if they can custom brand the product.

When buying from Alibaba, you'll need to buy in bulk, in order to have reasonable profit margins. So clear some space in your garage, and make sure you order test samples before buying a gigantic shipment.

Ok, so I've found a cool product. Now what?

Now it's time to build your website and your brand. For starters, you're going to need a catchy name and a fantastic logo. If you've never designed a logo before, I'd recommend getting a professional to design it for you. You can find logo designers on fivver.com for five bucks.

You're also going to need to build a web store. To do this, I'd recommend using either wordpress and woo commerce or shopify. Shopify is definitely easier to use if you've never designed a website before. It's very user friendly, however there are slightly more fees than woo commerce and wordpress.

It will probably take you a couple of hours to learn how to setup a web store, but I can assure you, it's not as complicated as you may think. In fact, setting up a wordpress shop is a lot like setting up a Facebook page. All you need to do is add content and upload photos, and the theme takes care of the rest of the work. If you get confused, be sure to watch some youtube tutorials, as there are countless videos out there with valuable information.

If you don't have time to worry about setting up a web store, you can always hire a professional from various freelance websites such as odesk.

Retaining your Visitors

When trying to build a brand, the most important aspect is keeping in contact with your visitors. It's vitally important to have a Facebook page, a snapchat, and some sort of email list that will allow you to connect with your Instagram traffic.

Mail chimp is a great website for building mailing lists. Make sure you give your visitors incentive when trying to grab their contact information. Give them 10% off if they enter their email, or do free giveaways if they like your Facebook page. Things like this really can go a long way.

Don't just use your own Instagram page

Once your web store has been built and is working properly, you should look into buying Instagram promotions and shoutouts from other Instagram accounts. The more hype you can create around your brand, the better it's going to do in the long run. Also invest in facebook ads, as you can specifically target people that would potentially be interested in your product.

Promoting Amazon Products

If you don't want to put in the time and effort to create your own web store, you can always simply list your product on amazon or ebay, and send your Instagram traffic to those websites.

This will greatly boost your ranking on amazon, and will create even more traffic and visitors that will buy your product or products. For example, let's say that 20 people from your Instagram traffic buy your product on Amazon. Amazon will recognize this, and will put your product on their first page under certain key words. Because Amazon does this, you will then get an additional 30 sales that come from Amazon's traffic alone. So with Amazon and Instagram working together, you can really make your product go viral.

It's definitely worth it to look into Amazon's FBA program, as they will take shipments directly from websites like Alibaba.

Affiliate Products

Using Instagram with affiliate marketing and affiliate websites is also a very powerful strategy.

What are affiliate products?

Affiliate products are simply products that you promote and get a commission on. So if you're promoting apple laptops, and you sell 3 that cost $1000 you will make $300 if you make a 10% commission on each sale.

Affiliate products work wonderfully if the products you are promoting via Instagram are expensive. This is because you'll make larger commissions on more expensive products.

An example of this is with a luxury fashion page. If you choose to run a luxury fashion page on Instagram, and build an audience of potential buyers that are wealthy and are looking to spend money, you will do very well. All you would have to do is create a website that has affiliate links to expensive/luxury clothing items.

If you sell 1 ten thousand dollar Rolex watch to one of your Instagram followers, you will make a whopping $1000 from one single sale. If your page has 100k wealthy luxury followers, you could potentially make millions a year from that one affiliate website. Obviously I'm being optimistic, but I just wanted to give you an idea how powerful affiliate marketing can be.

What's even better is that most affiliate programs have what's called a cookie. A cookie basically means that if someone clicks on your affiliate link through Instagram, and comes back to the website to buy the product 20 days later, you'll still get a commission. So people have up to a month in some cases to buy the product.

To find out if a product or brand has an affiliate marketing option, scroll down to the bottom of their website and look for an affiliate area. I'd say 75% of all large companies or websites have an affiliate sign up area.

A great place to checkout is commission junction. They directly connect you with thousands of companies that offer affiliate marketing and commissions. Another fantastic source is simply Amazon. Amazon has the largest affiliate network on the internet and pays thousands of affiliates each and every month.

Etsy

If you're into making handmade or vintage goods, definitely check out Etsy. It's a gigantic market place that is solely designed for selling custom made products.

If you have a jewellery or fashion Instagram page, Etsy should probably be your first go to. You can easily rank on google simply by creating a powerful Etsy listing with a detailed description. And just like Amazon, the more sales your Etsy products make, the better you will rank on their website.

Apps

Phone apps can be extremely profitable in the long run if you can promote them properly with Instagram. Before being intimidated with phone apps, remember that you can easily get them designed to your specific qualifications.

Personally, I have no app coding knowledge whatsoever, and rely entirely on app developers to bring my ideas to life.

If you're looking for someone to design an app for you, be sure to check out upwork.com. They have thousands of app developers that are hungry for work.

From my personal experience, the most successful apps that I have promoted on my Instagram pages have been apps that are directly related to my page's niche. Also, games apps are particularly hard to advertise on Instagram unless you Instagram page is catered towards gamers. When thinking about app ideas, try to think of an app that somehow solves people's problems. If you run an off-road trucks page, develop an app that gives people access to off road trails and logging roads. If you run a music related page, develop a guitar tuner app that has some sort of twist that makes it superior to other apps.

Another niche that works really well with phone apps is photography. If you run a photography page, you should look into developing an app that somehow uniquely lets you edit pictures. Maybe its vintage filters, collages or lighting effects. People go crazy over editing their pictures, which is why a photography app might be a fantastic option.

One of the most successful apps I've seen promoted was a puppy lover's dating application. It's basically an app that brings single people with dogs together. For a small subscription fee, people could meet up in person, walk their dogs, and connect with each other all through this simple dating app. It was promoted on many of the large pet Instagram pages and was extremely successful.

A great way to promote your app is to do giveaways. In the case of the puppy app, a smart idea might be to give away a luxury dog collar, on condition that your followers download and rate your application. The more positive ratings your app gets, the better it will do in the app store.

Stock Photography

Are you a photographer? Is your Instagram page a photography based page? If so, stock photography is definitely something that you should look into.

Anyone that uses photos for commercial purposes needs to buy stock photos for content. This includes blogs, ebooks, websites, and even YouTube videos.

Some great websites that you should look into are istockphoto, shutterstock, and fotolia. All you need to do is upload your collection of photos, tag them properly, and these websites will do all of the marketing and selling for you.

You get paid in royalties each and every month. One of the reasons why I love stock photography so much is because it is passive income. Even if you go on vacation for a month, shutterstock will continue selling your portfolio of photos, paying you awesome royalties.

Instagram can be a powerful way to promote your stock photography business. If people on Instagram love your photos and want to use them in their work, you can easily make sales using stock photography.

Another option is to sell your photos as prints. There are various websites out there that allow you to upload your photos, and sell them as prints online directly to your customers. You don't even need to touch the print, the website will ship all of your artwork directly to the customers via drop shipping.

Depending on the quality of your photos, you could potentially sell large prints of your work for $500 and more! People spend ridiculous amounts on artwork if they feel a connection with the artist. Instagram is a fantastic way to build that connection.

With products like artwork, it's always a good idea to have an incentive behind your work. Charity is an excellent option. Let your Instagram followers know that for every print you sell, you'll donate 20% of the profits to charity. Not only will you be helping people, you'll also double your sales by making your product a charitable item.

Clickbank

I've seen many quotes and business pages on Instagram selling Clickbank products. Clickbank products are basically a collection of videos or ebooks that teach you how to do a certain task.

An example of a Clickbank product is "How to make 100k flipping real estate." They're usually video courses that you can earn a commission on. Every time you make a sale, you can earn between $20 to $50 depending on how expensive the original price is.

Clickbank products work great on fitness pages, business pages, and even luxury pages. Even if you're unsure about Clickbank, head over to their website and checkout the various products they offer. You'll be surprised at how many courses are relatable to your niche.

If you have a puppy Instagram page, you can sell a Clickbank course teaching people how to train their new puppy via clicker training. All you need to do is leave the Clickbank link in your bio, and send people over to the course's landing page. Every time you sell the course, you'll make around $30.

Once you get potential customers on the landing page, the Clickbank courses take over for you. Often times, these Clickbank courses will have very convincing videos that entice people to buy their products. All you need to do is get your followers onto those landing pages.

The best part about Clickbank is that most of the courses are extremely high quality. People on Instagram will even specifically thank you for sending them to that specific course. They're almost always packed full of information, and taught by experts and professionals.

Adsense

If you're posting viral, humours content on a funny themed Instagram page, you may want to look into Google Adsense. Adsense is a very simple way to easily monetize your website or blog. The more traffic you can send to your website, the more you will make on adsense.

If you run a humour page on Instagram, try posting a short clip on your Instagram page with a caption like: "watch the full video on my website, buzzdaily.com" or something to that extent. You want to post interesting articles and videos that make people click on over to your website out of sheer curiosity.

I'm sure you've seen Facebook posts on your news feed that completely draw in your attention. Titles like: "Huge shark attacks whale." Then, when you click on the image, you're instantly taken over to their website that has ads surrounding the video.

This method also works on Instagram if done correctly. In the example of a humor page, you could post viral stand up comedy or vines in which you only post a short clip of the full video. In the description, simply write, "Watch the full video for free at BuzzVids.com."

This method should be your last resort, in case all other methods don't work. This is because people tend to get annoyed if you're constantly using "click bait" to get them over to your website. It is a working method however, which is why I included it in my book.

CPA Networks

This one can be a little tricky, which is why I included it as the last option for monetizing Instagram. CPA stands for "cost per action" which basically means that you get paid every time someone enters their email, phone number, or postal code.

Companies will pay you between $1 to $20 for people to sign up for the website or download an application.

A popular example of this is with dating websites. Many dating websites will pay you $1 to $2 for every person you can get to sign up on their dating website. So if you have an Instagram page that caters towards romance, relationships, or single people, you might want to look into CPA offers.

A great website to checkout is called CPAlead. They even have what's called content lockers which force people to complete a CPA offer if they want to watch a particular video, or download a certain link.

Chapter 11: Expanding your Assets

It's easy to get caught up in monetizing your Instagram account once you begin to generate a large following of people.

If a monetizing method is hurting your Instagram account growth, you should probably stop what you're doing, and focus entirely on growth. It's always better to expand now, and make money later. If you start to sellout your account too early, it's possible that you could completely blow and ruin all the progress you've made thus far.

In fact, I'd even go as far as to say that you should wait until you have 200k followers before you really start to attempt serious monetization. It's fine to sell some shoutouts here and there, but for the most part, you'll be better off if you focus entirely on growing your followers and your content. I know that it sounds crazy to go an entire year or so without monetizing, but I can promise you that it will be worth it in the end.

If you have one large Instagram account, you should definitely looking into starting a second, that is somewhat related to your first page. Give your second page shoutouts, and start growing your second page as fast as possible.

The more Instagram pages you have, the more sturdy your Instagram empire will be.

Another great idea is to move your followers away from Instagram, and onto other websites. Youtube and snapchat are great examples of this. I've seen many large

Instagram accounts promoting youtube videos in their bios and descriptions.

Even if you send 5k views to a youtube video, youtube will see this as a positive sign, and will start growing your videos for you, organically. In fact, I've seen Instagram pages with only 300k followers promo a youtube video all the way up to one million views.

Not only will you gain youtube subscribers, but you will also be able to monetize your youtube videos with google Adsense ads. (The ads you see before the video starts).

Also, you don't need to be some charismatic person to start a Youtube channel. You can simply post clips that you find on Instagram. Let's say for example you run a truck related Instagram page. A wise idea would be to start a Youtube channel that posts short clips of off roading truck videos. You can find thousands of these type of videos on Instagram if you search for certain hashtags. So in short, you don't even need to make the content! All you need to do is put a bunch of short clips together, and perhaps add some royalty free music in the background. Overtime, these videos will begin to rank on Youtube itself, and you will make money on autopilot month after month from Youtube.

Snapchat

Once you start growing rapidly on Instagram, I highly advise you to start sending people over to a Snapchat page.

Snapchat is going to be the most powerful tool in the next couple of years. Because posts only last 24 hours, people feel the need and the urgency to check all of their Snapchat updates. This basically guarantees that whatever you post, will be seen.

Even if you have a couple thousand followers on Snapchat, that's a couple thousand people that could potentially see your service or product directly from you.

If you run a puppy page on Instagram, and send people over to your Snapchat, you can easily advertise the products from your web store on Snapchat. Are you selling glow in the dark dog collars? Perfect, simply record some video of the collars for your snap story, and watch the sales roll in. It's a super powerful tool for marketing, perhaps even more powerful than Instagram itself.

Chapter 12: A Word of

Warning

Throughout your Instagram journey you will encounter people that will offer you large amounts of money for your Instagram pages. Do not do business with them.

I've even had one person offer as much as $50k via a bank transfer.

My advice to you, is never sell out. Your Instagram page will be twice as valuable in a year's time and you will be able to generate much more money than what people will offer.

You also never know who you're dealing with. You could be talking to scam artists or even skilled hackers. Stay away from these people, and always reject money offers. Don't even negotiate or leave selling your Instagram page on the table.

Email Scams

Also be careful what you are downloading in email attachments. If someone is sending you a video for a shoutout, get them to send it to you via KIK or another messaging system. Email can be dangerous as people can send viruses and keyloggers through email attachments.

(keyloggers are basically programs that hackers use to snatch your passwords).

Conclusion:

First of all, I'd like to thank you for taking the time to read my book. I hope it unlocked any barriers that stood in your way from making money on Instagram.

As a final word, I'd like to remind you to always invest in knowledge. Always be constantly learning because the online world changes constantly at a rapid rate. The quicker you can stay ahead, the more money you will make in the future by a long run.

Keep your eyes open for the latest trends, and have a solid network of people.

<u>*Before you go*</u>

If you found my book effective and useful, please remember to give me a good rating on Amazon!

If you have any constructive criticism, please email me before leaving a negative review. I always read emails that are sent my way, and will do anything I can to make this book better.

You can contact me here, on my Facebook page: Dave Wells

Have a great day, and thanks for reading.

Made in the USA
Lexington, KY
05 September 2018